C000170499

# You're
# Mer
# mazing

summersdale

YOU'RE MERMAZING

An Hachette UK Company
www.hachette.co.uk

Summersdale Publishers Ltd
Part of Octopus Publishing Group Limited
Carmelite House
50 Victoria Embankment
LONDON
EC4Y 0DZ
UK

www.summersdale.com

Printed and bound in the Czech Republic

ISBN: 978-1-78685-750-7

Substantial discounts on bulk quantities of Summersdale books are available to corporations, professional associations and other organisations. For details contact general enquiries: telephone: +44 (0) 1243 771107 or email: enquiries@summersdale.com.

TO.......................................

FROM................................

Trust yourself;
believe that you
have a unique
destiny to fulfil.

CANDY PAULL

*I have no fear of depths and a great fear of shallow living.*

ANAÏS NIN

It is confidence in our bodies, minds and spirits that allows us to keep looking for new adventures.

OPRAH WINFREY

# SHIMMER AND SHINE YOUR WAY THROUGH LIFE

YOU HAVE
TO BELIEVE IN
YOURSELF OR NO
ONE ELSE WILL.

SARAH MICHELLE
GELLAR

*Never dull your shine
for somebody else.*

TYRA BANKS

Mythical
soulmate:
mermaid

The most
courageous act
is still to think
for yourself.
Aloud.

COCO CHANEL

When you know
yourself, you are
empowered. When
you accept yourself,
you are invincible.

TINA LIFFORD

# FEELING
# FINTASTIC

I don't like to gamble, but if there's one thing I'm willing to bet on, it's myself.

**BEYONCÉ**

*Always be a
first-rate version
of yourself, instead of
a second-rate version
of somebody else.*

JUDY GARLAND

when you have
confidence, you can
have a lot of fun.

JOE NAMATH

# SING,
# SPLASH,
# SPARKLE

THE OCEAN STIRS
THE HEART, INSPIRES
THE IMAGINATION
AND BRINGS ETERNAL
JOY TO THE SOUL.

ROBERT WYLAND

*Anything is possible once you believe you are worthy of achieving it.*

JASON POCKRANDT

Be a
mermaid
in a school
of fish

Nothing can
dim the light that
shines from within.

MAYA ANGELOU

When you discover
something that
nourishes your soul...
care enough about
yourself to make room
for it in your life.

JEAN SHINODA BOLEN

Once you choose hope, anything is possible.

CHRISTOPHER REEVE

# BORN WILD
# AND FREE

My soul is full of longing
for the secret of the sea,

And the heart of the
great ocean

sends a thrilling pulse
through me.

HENRY WADSWORTH LONGFELLOW

*Don't let them tame you.*

ISADORA DUNCAN

# ALWAYS BELIEVE
# AND YOU'LL
# ALWAYS ACHIEVE

IN STILL MOMENTS
BY THE SEA, LIFE
SEEMS LARGE-DRAWN
AND SIMPLE. IT IS
THERE WE CAN SEE
INTO OURSELVES.

ROLF EDBERG

*Just be yourself –*
*there is no one better.*

TAYLOR SWIFT

# Unfold
# your own
# myth.

RUMI

Your
sparkle has
not gone
unnoticed

We have to dare
to be ourselves,
however frightening
or strange that self
may prove to be.

MAY SARTON

Those who don't
believe in magic
will never find it.

ROALD DAHL

BE FOREVER
MAGICAL

*To love oneself is the beginning of a lifelong romance.*

**OSCAR WILDE**

Look at that sea, girls...
we couldn't enjoy its
loveliness any more if we
had millions of dollars
and ropes of diamonds.

L. M. MONTGOMERY

ONCE WE BELIEVE
IN OURSELVES, WE CAN
RISK CURIOSITY, WONDER,
SPONTANEOUS DELIGHT,
OR ANY EXPERIENCE
THAT REVEALS THE
HUMAN SPIRIT.

E. E. CUMMINGS

Release
your
inner mermaid

*The world's finest wilderness lies beneath the waves.*

ROBERT WYLAND

# Talk to yourself like you would to someone you love.

BRENÉ BROWN

# WHY BE NORMAL WHEN YOU CAN BE SOMETHING OUT OF THIS WORLD?

Dare to be different and to set your own pattern; live your own life and follow your own star.

WILFERD PETERSON

To be yourself
in a world that is
constantly trying to
make you something
else is the greatest
accomplishment.

RALPH WALDO EMERSON

*I am longing to be
with you, and by the
sea, where we can talk
together freely and build
our castles in the air.*

**BRAM STOKER**

# BE BRAVE AND
# MAKE WAVES

OPTIMISM IS THE
FAITH THAT LEADS
TO ACHIEVEMENT.
NOTHING CAN BE
DONE WITHOUT HOPE
AND CONFIDENCE.

HELEN KELLER

You are magnificent
beyond measure,
perfect in your
imperfections and
wonderfully made.

ABIOLA ABRAMS

All you need is a bit of Vitamin sea

*If you're presenting yourself with confidence, you can pull off pretty much anything.*

**KATY PERRY**

You're awake,
you're awesome.
Live like it.

ROBBY NOVAK

Do not doubt the
goodness in you.

DODINSKY

# MERMAID
# KISSES
# AND
# STARFISH
# WISHES

If you are going
to doubt something,
doubt your limits.

DON WARD

*You need to believe in yourself and what you do. Be tenacious and genuine.*

**CHRISTIAN LOUBOUTIN**

# WHY SINK WHEN
# YOU CAN SWIM?

# be unapologetically you.

STEVE MARABOLI

Follow your inner
moonlight; don't
hide the madness.

ALLEN GINSBERG

The greatest doer
must also be a
great dreamer.

THEODORE
ROOSEVELT

Don't let anyone burst your bubble

LOVE YOURSELF
FIRST AND
EVERYTHING ELSE
FALLS INTO LINE.

LUCILLE BALL

Expand your dreams...
dare to tap into
your greatness.

ROBIN SHARMA

CALM SEAS NEVER
MADE SKILLED
MERMAIDS

Dreams are
free therapy.

TERRI GUILLEMETS

It ain't what they call you, it's what you answer to.

W. C. FIELDS

Wherever
you go, go with
all your heart.

CONFUCIUS

# WORK HARD TODAY, SPLASH AROUND TOMORROW

No pessimist ever
discovered the secrets
of the stars, or sailed
to an uncharted land,
or opened a new heaven
to the human spirit.

HELEN KELLER

*Capture your dreams and your life becomes full. You can, because you think you can.*

**NIKITA KOLOFF**

# TO DO:
## shimmer and
## sparkle

Don't be pushed by your problems; be led by your dreams.

RALPH WALDO EMERSON

To accomplish great
things, we must not
only act, but also
dream; not only plan,
but also believe.

ANATOLE FRANCE

The heart of man is very much like the sea: it has its storms, it has its tides and in its depths it has its pearls too.

VINCENT VAN GOGH

# SEAS THE DAY

DREAMS ARE
ILLUSTRATIONS...
FROM THE BOOK YOUR
SOUL IS WRITING
ABOUT YOU.

MARSHA NORMAN

*Whatever you can do,
or dream you can, begin
it. Boldness has genius,
power and magic in it.*

**JOHANN WOLFGANG
VON GOETHE**

# MAKE EVERY DAY
# MORE MAGICAL

Do not be
embarrassed by
your failures.
Learn from them
and start again.

RICHARD BRANSON

Never give up on a dream just because of the time it will take to accomplish it. The time will pass anyway.

EARL
NIGHTINGALE

Life is a sea of vibrant colour. Jump in.

A. D. POSEY

Swim
through life
like a
mermaid

Life isn't about
finding yourself.
Life is about
creating yourself.

GEORGE BERNARD SHAW

why fit in when
you were born
to stand out?

DR SEUSS

# HIGH TIDES =
# GOOD VIBES

SHOOT FOR THE
MOON. EVEN IF YOU
MISS, YOU'LL LAND
AMONG THE STARS.

NORMAN VINCENT PEALE

*Follow your dreams,*
*work hard, practise*
*and persevere.*

SASHA COHEN

You protect your
being when you
Love yourself better.
That's the secret.

ISABELLE ADJANI

# MAKE YOUR WISHES AND DREAMS YOUR REALITY

I believe in writing
your own story.

CHARLOTTE ERIKSSON

The sigh of all the
seas breaking in
measure round the
isles soothed them.

VIRGINIA WOOLF

Be as
free as
the ocean

# If you can dream it, you can do it.

TOM FITZGERALD

Our aspirations
are our possibilities.

PUT YOUR EAR DOWN
CLOSE TO YOUR SOUL
AND LISTEN HARD.

ANNE SEXTON

# BE YOUR OWN
## KIND OF
## BEAUTIFUL

*What we do flows from who we are.*

PAUL VITALE

It is not wrong
to be different.
sometimes it
is hard, but it
is not wrong.

ELIZABETH MOON

# WHERE THERE'S
# A WILL,
# THERE'S A WAVE

The sea is as near
as we come to
another world.

ANNE STEVENSON

*Laugh often,*
*dream big, reach*
*for the stars!*

ANONYMOUS

Shell
yeah!

A full moon sprinkled
the black ocean with
diamonds and she could
imagine fairies dancing in
the silver foam that laced
the huge, dark waves.

PATRICIA HAGAN

We ask ourselves, who
am I to be brilliant,
gorgeous, handsome,
talented and fabulous?
Actually, who are
you not to be?

MARIANNE WILLIAMSON

# NOT ALL STARS
# ARE IN THE SKY

IT'S THE SOUND
OF THE SEA THAT
MAKES YOU BELIEVE
IN MERMAIDS.

ANTHONY T. HINCKS

*Be yourself.*
*The world worships*
*the original.*

INGRID BERGMAN

Reach high, for stars
lie hidden in your
soul. Dream deep,
for every dream
precedes the goal.

PAMELA VAULL STARR

# UNIQUENESS IS
# WHAT MAKES
# YOU BEAUTIFUL

There is no chance,
no destiny, no fate,
Can circumvent or
hinder or control
The firm resolve of a
determined soul.

ELLA WHEELER WILCOX

*In dreams...
there are no
impossibilities.*

JÁNOS ARANY

Always
be yourself
unless you can
be a mermaid

To me the sea is a
continual miracle,
The fishes that swim
– the rocks – the
motion of the waves.

WALT WHITMAN

Be brave enough
to live creatively...
what you'll discover
will be wonderful.
What you'll discover
will be yourself.

ALAN ALDA

DO NOT FORGET
YOUR DUTY TO
LOVE YOURSELF.

SØREN KIERKEGAARD

DAZZLE THEM
WITH YOUR
INNER BEAUTY

*I am whoever
I say I am.*

AMERICA FERRERA

Your greatest self has been waiting your whole life; don't make it wait any longer.

STEVE MARABOLI

# CHASE WAVES
# EVERY SINGLE DAY

Just when the
caterpillar thought
the world was
ending, it became
a butterfly.

**PROVERB**

*Be in love
with your life,
every detail of it.*

JACK KEROUAC

Be fierce,
free and
fabulous

without leaps of
imagination, or
dreaming, we lose
the excitement
of possibilities.

GLORIA STEINEM

The most important
kind of freedom
is to be what you
really are.

JIM MORRISON

# ALWAYS ACT LIKE YOU'RE WEARING AN INVISIBLE CROWN

IF I AM NOT
FOR MYSELF,
WHO IS FOR ME?

HILLEL THE ELDER

*Live in the sunshine,*
*swim the sea,*
*Drink the wild*
*air's salubrity.*

RALPH WALDO
EMERSON

The final forming
of a person's
character lies in
their own hands.

ANNE FRANK

# NEVER LOSE SIGHT
# OF YOUR DREAMS

It takes courage
to grow up and
become who you
really are.

E. E. CUMMINGS

*You have to be unique and different, and shine in your own way.*

LADY GAGA

Dreams are
the playgrounds
of mermaids

Your self-worth
is defined by you.
You don't have
to depend on
someone telling
you who you are.

BEYONCÉ

It's not selfish to
love yourself, take
care of yourself
and to make your
happiness a priority.
It's a necessity.

MANDY HALE

OWNING OUR STORY... IS THE BRAVEST THING THAT WE WILL EVER DO.

BRENÉ BROWN

# BIRTHSTONE:
# AQUAMARINE

How you love
yourself is how
you teach others
to love you.

**RUPI KAUR**

We become happier,
much happier, when
we realise life is an
opportunity rather
than an obligation.

MARY AUGUSTINE

# I WASHED UP
# LIKE THIS

Believe in yourself...
Know that there is
something inside
you that is greater
than any obstacle.

CHRISTIAN D. LARSON

We should stop
defining each other by
what we are not, and
start defining ourselves
by what we are.

EMMA WATSON

You can be the ripest, juiciest peach in the world, and there's still going to be somebody who hates peaches.

DITA VON TEESE

# Be more
# mermaid

WHOEVER
IS HAPPY WILL
MAKE OTHERS
HAPPY TOO.

ANNE FRANK

Instead of... focusing on
your flaws, look in the
mirror and appreciate
your best features...
everyone has them.

DEMI LOVATO

SHINE BRIGHT
AND THE WHOLE
WORLD SHINES
WITH YOU

*In one drop of water
are found all the
secrets of all the
endless oceans.*

**KAHLIL GIBRAN**

To be beautiful means
to be yourself. You don't
need to be accepted
by others. You need
to accept yourself.

THÍCH NHẤT HANH

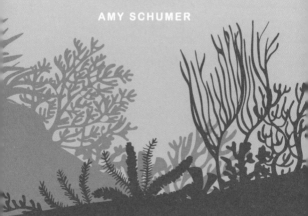

I say if I'm beautiful.
I say if I'm strong.
You will not
determine my
story – I will.

**AMY SCHUMER**

I LOVE THE PERSON
I WAS BORN TO BE

*I'm a big believer
in accepting yourself
the way you are
and not really
worrying about it.*

JENNIFER
LAWRENCE

# Attitude is everything.

DIANE VON FÜRSTENBERG

IT IS ADVISABLE
TO LOOK FROM
THE TIDE POOL TO
THE STARS AND
THEN BACK TO THE
TIDE POOL AGAIN.

JOHN STEINBECK

Ignore self-doubt
and inner conflict.
Dwell on positive
thoughts.

LAILAH GIFTY AKITA

*No one can make
you feel inferior
without your consent.*

**ELEANOR ROOSEVELT**

Go confidently in the direction of your dreams. Live the life you have imagined.

HENRY DAVID THOREAU

keep shining,
beautiful one.
The world needs
your light.

ANONYMOUS

JUST REMEMBER:
YOU'RE MERMAZING

# Image Credits

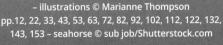

If you're interested in finding
out more about our books,
find us on Facebook at
summersdale publishers
and follow us on Twitter
at @summersdale.

www.summersdale.com